mathematics

FOR LEARNING

Measuring for the Art Show

Addition on the Open Number Line

Catherine Twomey Fosnot

firsthand
An imprint of Heinemann
A division of Reed Elsevier, Inc.
361 Hanover Street
Portsmouth, NH 03801–3912
firsthand.heinemann.com

Offices and agents throughout the world

ISBN 13: 978-0-325-01010-6
ISBN 10: 0-325-01010-2

Harcourt School Publishers
6277 Sea Harbor Drive
Orlando, FL 32887–6777
www.harcourtschool.com

ISBN 13: 978-0-15-360562-8
ISBN 10: 0-15-360562-6

© 2007 Catherine Twomey Fosnot

The development of a portion of the material described within was supported in part by the National Science Foundation under Grant No. 9911841. Any opinions, findings, and conclusions or recommendations expressed in these materials are those of the authors and do not necessarily reflect the views of the National Science Foundation.

Library of Congress Cataloging-in-Publication Data
CIP data is on file with the Library of Congress

Printed in the United States of America on acid-free paper

15 14 13 12 11   CGX   2 3 4 5 6

Acknowledgements

Literacy Consultant

Nadjwa E.L. Norton
Childhood Education, City College of New York

Photography

Herbert Seignoret
Mathematics in the City, City College of New York

Illustrator

Meryl Treatner

Schools featured in photographs:

The Muscota New School/PS 314 (an empowerment school in Region 10), New York, NY
Independence School/PS 234 (Region 9), New York, NY
Fort River Elementary School, Amherst, MA

Contents

Unit Overview

The focus of this unit is the development of the open number line model within the context of measurement. As the unit progresses, the number line is used as a model for double-digit addition strategies. The unit begins with the story of a teacher who has offered to organize an art show of children's work as a school fund-raiser. The children have produced beautiful pieces of art and the teacher and several children set out to make signs to hang underneath each piece, listing the title of the piece, the artist's name, and the price. They want to measure each art piece very carefully so that the sign will be exactly the same length as the piece of art. But this huge pile of work is daunting. Thankfully, the students soon figure out a solution. They sort the art by size, measure each size, and make a blueprint—a pattern strip—that will be used for cutting all the signs.

The story sets the context for a series of investigations in this unit. Children measure various sizes of art paper with connecting cubes and then place the measurements onto a long strip of adding machine paper, to be used as a blueprint or pattern for cutting the signs. As the unit progresses, lengths of five

The Landscape of Learning

BIG IDEAS

- ☀ Distance is measured as a series of iterated units
- ☀ Units used in measuring can vary in size, but the results will be equivalent
- ☀ Numbers can be decomposed and the subunits or smaller amounts can be added in varying orders, yet still be equivalent
- ☀ There are place value patterns that occur when adding on groups of ten
- ☀ Unitizing

STRATEGIES

- ☀ Counting three times
- ☀ Counting on
- ☀ Using the five- and ten-structures
- ☀ Keeping one number whole, using landmark numbers, and/or taking leaps of ten
- ☀ Splitting

MODEL

- ☀ Open number line

and ten are introduced in place of the cubes and the blueprint is progressively developed into an open number line—a helpful model used as a tool to explore and represent strategies for double-digit addition.

In contrast to a number line with counting numbers written below, an "open" number line is just an empty line used to record children's addition (and later subtraction) strategies. Only the numbers children use are recorded and the addition is recorded as leaps or jumps. For example, if a child's strategy for adding 18 + 79 is to keep 79 whole and decompose the 18 into smaller pieces, moving to a landmark number of 80 (79 + 1 + 10 + 7), it would be recorded on the open number line like this:

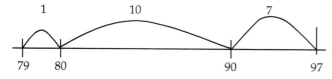

Such representations help children move beyond tedious strategies like counting on by ones to strategies such as taking leaps of ten, splitting, and using landmark numbers.

Several minilessons for addition are also included in the unit. These are structured as strings of related problems designed to guide learners more explicitly toward computational fluency with double-digit addition.

The unit culminates with an art show. Thus, as you progress through the unit, you may find it helpful to work with the art teacher in your school to collect pieces of student artwork.

The Mathematical Landscape

Research has documented that different models have different effects on mental computation strategies: base-ten blocks may support the development of the standard algorithms, while the hundred chart supports the development of strategies such as counting by tens. The open number line better aligns with children's invented strategies and it stimulates a mental representation of numbers and number operations that is more powerful for developing mental arithmetic strategies (Beishuizen 1993; Gravemeijer 1991). Students using the open number line are cognitively involved in their actions. In contrast, students who use

base-ten blocks or the hundred chart tend to depend primarily on visualization, which results in a passive "reading off" behavior rather than cognitive involvement in the actions undertaken (Klein, Beishuizen, and Treffers 2002). This unit develops the open number line as a model for double-digit addition. It also supports the development of several big ideas and strategies for addition along the way.

BIG IDEAS

This unit is designed to encourage the development of some of the big ideas underlying early number sense, measurement, and addition:

❖ *distance is measured as a series of iterated units*

❖ *units used in measuring can vary in size, but the results will be equivalent*

❖ *numbers can be decomposed and the subunits or smaller amounts can be added in varying orders, yet still be equivalent (associative and commutative properties)*

❖ *there are place value patterns that occur when adding on groups of ten*

❖ *unitizing*

❖ Distance is measured as a series of iterated units

Young children may think that when measuring only the last unit matters, as that is where you make a mark. They may not realize that the distance is comprised of a collection of units, side by side, spanning a length. As children measure, it is important to notice if they carefully place the first unit at the beginning and count it as one. Also, do they think the mark can be anywhere on the last cube (since that is a total amount) or do they realize it is the edge of the cube that matters (since each cube represents a unit of distance, not just an amount)?

❖ Units used in measuring can vary in size, but the results will be equivalent

Distance can be measured with various units—for example, connecting cubes or strips of ten. Although the results of the measuring may be different, they are equivalent. For example, 25 cubes is equivalent to a distance of five groups of five cubes or two groups of ten and one group of five. It is also equivalent to two and a half strips of ten. Initially, this idea may be difficult for children to understand. Thus, it is important to engage children in measuring a variety of lengths with a collection of single units and then to group the units and transpose these lengths onto strips, which can also be used as a measurement length. By moving back and forth from units to groups to strips of distance and discussing these issues, children begin to construct an understanding of what it means to measure a length.

❖ Numbers can be decomposed and the subunits or smaller amounts can be added in varying orders, yet still be equivalent (associative and commutative properties)

With previous units in this series (for example, see *Bunk Beds and Apple Boxes*), as children developed strategies for addition, they may have constructed the idea of compensation—that if you lose one (from five, for example) but gain it (onto three), the total stays the same: $5 + 3 = 4 + 4$. In this unit, ideas about decomposing, arranging, and rearranging are deepened as children work with greater numbers—double-digits—and are supported to make use of the five- and ten-structures to develop efficient addition strategies. The associative property allows for decomposing and composing: $38 + 17 = 38 + (2 + 15) = (38 + 2) + 15$. The commutative property allows for adding in a different order: $38 + 17 = 17 + 38$.

❖ There are place value patterns that occur when adding on groups of ten

Once children have an understanding of the landmark decade numbers in our number system, they can easily count forward by ten: 10, 20, 30, etc. But adding 10 onto a number when the unit amount is not 0 (e.g., 32) is often another story. Children are frequently surprised by the pattern that results when one repeatedly adds ten—42, 52, 62, 72, etc. Knowledge of this pattern and why it occurs is an important big idea connected to place value that is also critical to the development of efficient addition strategies. For example, when solving $42 + 19$, we often wish children would just mentally think: 52, 62,

minus 1, 61. But without a deep knowledge of place value and the patterns that result when adding groups of ten, this is not an easy strategy. Although the focus of this unit is not on the development of an understanding of place value per se, several minilessons are included to explore and/or remind children of the patterns that result when adding tens. (The units in the series that focus more specifically on developing an understanding of place value are *Organizing and Collecting* and *The T-Shirt Factory*.)

❖ Unitizing

Unitizing requires that children use numbers to count not only objects but also groups—and to count them both simultaneously. For young learners, unitizing is a shift in perspective. Children have just learned to count ten objects, one by one. Unitizing these ten things as *one* thing—one group—challenges their original idea of a number. How can something be ten and one at the same time?

As children develop the ability to see five as a subunit you may begin to see them count the number of groups of five. For example, they may say fifteen is three groups of five. Here they are unitizing; they are treating the five as a group, counted as one—one group of five.

STRATEGIES

As you work with the activities in this unit, you will also see children use a variety of strategies for addition. Here are some strategies to notice:

❖ **counting three times**

❖ **counting on**

❖ **using the five- and ten-structures**

❖ **keeping one number whole, using landmark numbers, and/or taking leaps of ten**

❖ **splitting**

❖ Counting three times

Children's first attempts at addition usually involve counting. They count the objects in each group by ones and then count all over again from one to figure out the total. For example, to solve $33 + 18$, they make two groups—a group of 33 and a group of 18—counting by ones each time. They then combine the two groups and count the total, starting from one again.

❖ Counting on

Eventually children construct a counting-on strategy—they hold one amount in their minds and count the other amount on. For 33 + 18, they might start at 33 and then continue counting on, 34, 35, 36, . . . 51.

Although counting strategies may be very appropriate in the beginning of the development of addition, they are tedious strategies that leave many opportunities for losing track and other errors, particularly when children are working with double-digit numbers. Teachers often think a pencil and paper strategy with regrouping is the next step. This is not true. Children need to develop the ability to *look to the numbers first* and then decide on an appropriate strategy based on those particular numbers. In many cases pencil and paper are not needed.

❖ Using the five- and ten-structures

One of the most important ways of structuring a number is to compose and decompose amounts into groups of five and ten. For example, seeing 8 as 5 + 3, or 7 as 5 + 2, is very helpful in automatizing the basic fact "8 + 7." Since 3 + 2 also equals 5, 8 + 7 is equivalent to 3 fives. The five-structure is also helpful in automatizing all the combinations that make ten— if 6 is equivalent to 5 + 1, then only 4 more are needed to make 2 fives, which equals 10. Similarly it can be helpful to think of 7 + 8 as 3 fives, or 9 + 7 as 10 + 6.

❖ Keeping one number whole, using landmark numbers, and/or taking leaps of ten

As the big ideas for measurement and addition are being constructed, you will want to encourage children to use them for computation. One of the first strategies to encourage is using landmark numbers and taking leaps of ten. For example 33 + 29 can be solved like this: 43, 53, plus 7 to get to 60 (a landmark), plus 2 more. This strategy will eventually develop into the ability to add 29 by adding 30 − 1. The same problem, 33 + 29, can also be solved by turning it into 32 + 30 or by first adding 7 to 33 to get to the landmark number of 40 to get to an easier problem: 40 + 22. Having a deep understanding of landmark numbers and operations is the hallmark of computing with numeracy.

❖ Splitting

Another important strategy to encourage is splitting—decomposing by splitting the columns and making use of partial sums. For example, 33 + 29 can be solved as 30 + 20 + 3 + 9. Not only is this strategy important for mental arithmetic, it is also a precursor to the development of the place value algorithm (Kamii 1985).

It is important for you to notice these emerging strategies and celebrate children's developing number sense! A long-term objective on the horizon of the landscape of learning for addition is for children to look to the numbers first before deciding on a strategy. Mathematicians do not use the same strategy for every problem; their strategies vary depending on the numbers. Note when children begin to vary their strategies and search for efficiency. Knowing that this is OK to do, however, is based on understanding the big ideas of the commutative and associative properties and having a good sense of landmark numbers.

MATHEMATICAL MODELING

The model being developed in this unit is the open number line. With this model, children are supported to envision numbers as the magnitude of distances on a line, as equivalent quantities (composites of fives, tens, and ones), and by their proximity to landmark numbers. They are also able to explore representations of various addition strategies on the number line to support the development of various efficient strategies for computational fluency.

Models go through three stages of development (Gravemeijer 1999; Fosnot and Dolk 2001):

❖ *model of the situation*

❖ *model of children's strategies*

❖ *model as a tool for thinking*

❖ Model of the situation

Initially models grow out of children's attempts to model situations with drawings or connecting cubes. In this unit, the open number line emerges as a blueprint, a paper strip with marks on it for cutting. Initially the iterated units are cubes, but in time the five- and ten-structures are used.

❖ Model of children's strategies

Students benefit from seeing the teacher model their strategies. Once the model has emerged in the classroom community as a model of a situation, you can use it as a representational model as children explain their computation strategies. The open number line helps children envision and discuss actions for addition. If a child solves 33 + 18 by adding on 20 and removing 2, draw the following:

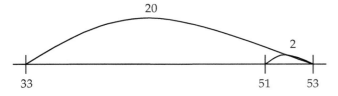

If a child says, "I made the problem friendly. I turned it into 31 + 20," draw the following:

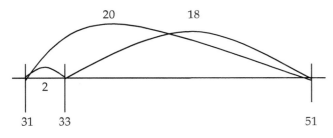

❖ Model as a tool for thinking

Eventually children will be able to use the open number line model as a tool to think with—to explore and prove the relationship between addition and subtraction, and to explore subtraction as removal and as difference.

Many opportunities to discuss these landmarks in mathematical development will arise as you work through this unit. Look for moments of puzzlement. Don't hesitate to let children discuss their ideas and check and recheck their strategies. Celebrate their accomplishments just as you would a toddler's first steps when learning to walk!

A graphic of the full landscape of learning for early number sense, addition, and subtraction is provided on page 11. The purpose of this graphic is to allow you to see the longer journey of children's mathematical development and to place your work in this unit within the scope of this long-term development. You may also find it helpful to use this graphic as a way to record the progress of individual children for yourself. Each landmark can be shaded in as you find evidence in a child's work and in what the child says—evidence that a landmark strategy, big idea, or way of modeling has been constructed. In a sense, you will be recording the individual pathways children take as they develop as young mathematicians!

References and Resources

Beishuizen, Meindert. 1993. Mental strategies and materials or models for addition and subtraction up to 100 in Dutch second grades. *Journal for Research in Mathematics Education, 24,* 294–323.

Dolk, Maarten and Catherine Twomey Fosnot. 2004a. *Addition and Subtraction Minilessons, Grades PreK–3.* CD-ROM with accompanying facilitator's guide by Antonia Cameron, Sherrin B. Hersch, and Catherine Twomey Fosnot. Portsmouth, NH: Heinemann.

———. 2004b. *Fostering Children's Mathematical Development, Grades PreK–3: The Landscape of Learning.* CD-ROM with accompanying facilitator's guide by Sherrin B. Hersch, Antonia Cameron, and Catherine Twomey Fosnot. Portsmouth, NH: Heinemann.

———. 2004c. *Working with the Number Line, Grades PreK–3: Mathematical Models.* CD-ROM with accompanying facilitator's guide by Antonia Cameron, Sherrin B. Hersch, and Catherine Twomey Fosnot. Portsmouth, NH: Heinemann.

Fosnot, Catherine Twomey and Maarten Dolk. 2001. *Young Mathematicians at Work: Constructing Number Sense, Addition, and Subtraction.* Portsmouth, NH: Heinemann.

Gravemeijer, Koeno P.E. 1991. An instruction-theoretical reflection on the use of manipulatives. In *Realistic Mathematics Education in Primary School,* ed. Leen Streefland. Utrecht, Netherlands: Freudenthal Institute.

———. 1999. How emergent models may foster the constitution of formal mathematics. *Mathematical Thinking and Learning, 1*(2), 155–77.

Kamii, Constance. 1985. *Young Children Reinvent Arithmetic.* New York, NY: Teachers College Press.

Karlin, Samuel. 1983. Eleventh R.A. Fisher Memorial Lecture. *Royal Society 20.*

Klein, Anton S., Meindert Beishuizen, and Adri Treffers. 2002. The empty number line in Dutch second grade, In *Lessons Learned from Research,* eds. Judith Sowder and Bonnie Schapelle. Reston, VA: National Council of Teachers of Mathematics.

NUMBER SENSE, ADDITION, and SUBTRACTION

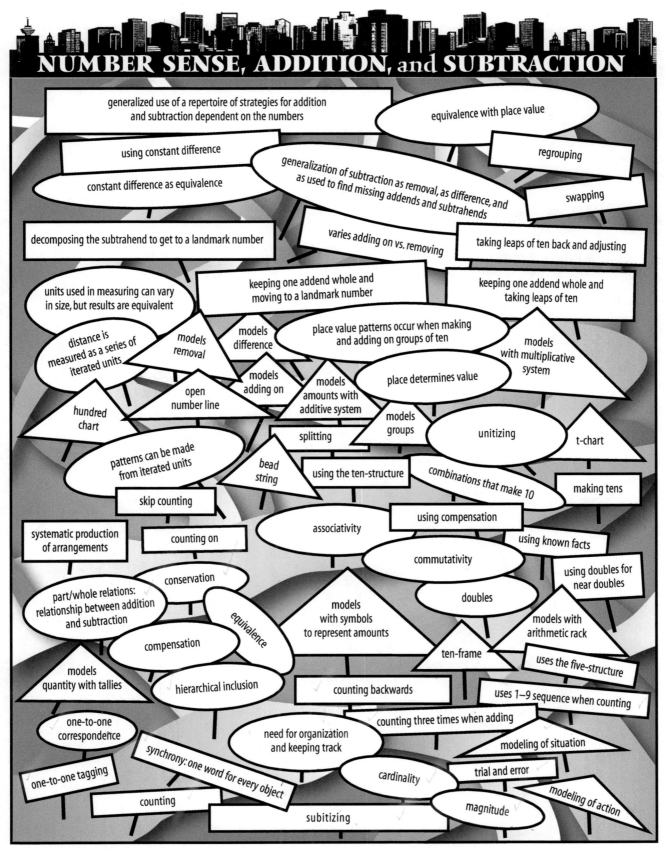

generalized use of a repertoire of strategies for addition and subtraction dependent on the numbers

equivalence with place value

using constant difference

regrouping

constant difference as equivalence

generalization of subtraction as removal, as difference, and as used to find missing addends and subtrahends

swapping

decomposing the subtrahend to get to a landmark number

varies adding on vs. removing

taking leaps of ten back and adjusting

units used in measuring can vary in size, but results are equivalent

keeping one addend whole and moving to a landmark number

keeping one addend whole and taking leaps of ten

distance is measured as a series of iterated units

models removal

models difference

place value patterns occur when making and adding on groups of ten

models with multiplicative system

hundred chart

open number line

models adding on

models amounts with additive system

place determines value

patterns can be made from iterated units

bead string

splitting

models groups

unitizing

t-chart

skip counting

using the ten-structure

combinations that make 10

making tens

systematic production of arrangements

counting on

associativity

using compensation

using known facts

commutativity

using doubles for near doubles

conservation

part/whole relations: relationship between addition and subtraction

equivalence

doubles

compensation

models with symbols to represent amounts

models with arithmetic rack

models quantity with tallies

hierarchical inclusion

ten-frame

uses the five-structure

counting backwards

uses 1–9 sequence when counting

one-to-one correspondence

need for organization and keeping track

counting three times when adding

modeling of situation

synchrony: one word for every object

cardinality

trial and error

one-to-one tagging

modeling of action

counting

magnitude

subitizing

The landscape of learning: number sense, addition, and subtraction on the horizon showing landmark strategies (rectangles), big ideas (ovals), and models (triangles).

DAY ONE
Measuring for the Art Show

Today you will develop the context, laying out the terrain for the work of the next few days. After listening to you read the book *Measuring for the Art Show,* the children prepare for their own art show by using connecting cubes to measure the lengths and widths of several types of art paper. As you move around the room supporting, encouraging, and conferring, you will notice various measurement strategies—these are the children's conceptions at the start of the unit.

Day One Outline

Developing the Context

☀ Read *Measuring for the Art Show* and discuss having an art show.

☀ Explain that children will need to measure the art paper so that they can make signs for the artwork.

Supporting the Investigation

☀ Have children work in pairs, measuring the art paper with cubes.

Preparing for the Math Congress

☀ Take note of the various measurement strategies and struggles you see and decide what to highlight during the math congress.

Materials Needed

Measuring for the Art Show [If you do not have a copy of the full-color read-aloud book (available from Heinemann), you can use Appendix A.]

Student recording sheet for the art paper investigation (Appendix B)—one per pair of children

Connecting cubes (sorted to include two colors only)—one bin per pair of children

Clipboards—one per pair of children

Large chart pad and easel (or chalkboard or whiteboard)

Markers

Several sheets each of colored art, chart, or poster paper, cut to the lengths listed on page 14.

Developing the Context

☀ Read *Measuring for the Art Show* and discuss having an art show.

☀ Explain that children will need to measure the art paper so that they can make signs for the artwork.

Note: Before class begins, cut several sheets of colored art, chart, or poster paper to the following lengths:

Blue: 14 cubes by 10 cubes
Purple: 22 cubes by 20 cubes
White: 35 cubes by 40 cubes
Chart paper: 46 cubes by 54 cubes
Yellow poster paper: 84 cubes by 60 cubes

It is important that the children are using the same manipulative that you used when measuring the papers for cutting. Some connecting cubes are three-quarter-inch and others are two centimeters. The paper colors are not important and can be changed, but you will want to make the colors listed on the recording sheet (Appendix B) correspond with the colors you use.

Read *Measuring for the Art Show* (Appendix A). When you finish reading the story, discuss with the children how clever it was to build the blueprint and how terrific it was that everyone in the story worked together.

Suggest that maybe your class could have an art show as well. As in the story, a sign will be needed for each piece of art. Explain that you want the signs to be *exactly as long as the pieces of art*. On a chart or the chalkboard, draw a picture like the following:

Behind the Numbers

The measurements for the papers to be cut have been carefully chosen for their relationship to multiples of five and ten (some are multiples; some are near multiples, being one or two away). As the unit progresses, these measurements will be placed on an emergent number line. At that point, alternating groups of five connecting cubes (two colors) will be provided as a support. If you do not have paper that you can cut to the exact measurements, other measurements can be used, but ensure that your numbers include 10 and 20 and span up to larger numbers close to 100. Also ensure that several measurements are one or two away from a multiple of five.

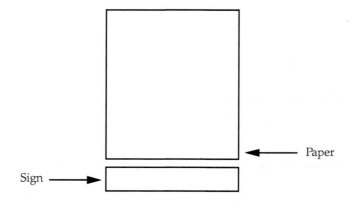

Ask the children to help you measure several sizes of paper and show them the variety you have prepared. Explain that you will put bins of connecting cubes at each table as tools to help in measuring.

Supporting the Investigation

Assign math partners and give each pair of children a clipboard and one recording sheet (Appendix B). Distribute several sheets of the cut paper at tables and on the floor to give children ample space to work. At each table, place bins of connecting cubes, sorted to include only two colors each. As children work, walk around and take note of the strategies you see. Confer with children as needed to support and challenge them. Do not show them how to measure. Instead, note their strategies and look for moments when you can encourage reflection and, if appropriate, puzzlement. At the end of the investigation, children should put their recording sheets in their work folders for use on Day Two.

☀ Have children work in pairs, measuring the art paper with cubes.

Appendix B	Student recording sheet for the art paper investigation
Name	Date
Blue paper:	
Short side	Long side
Purple paper:	
Short side	Long side
White paper:	
Short side	Long side
Chart paper:	
Short side	Long side
Yellow poster paper:	
Short side	Long side

Conferring with Children at Work

Inside One Classroom

Abbie: I think we should make the cubes into groups of 10 to keep track.

David: *(Makes groups of ten: ten blue, ten white, ten blue.)* It's not enough. We need more, 1, 2, 3, 4, 5. There—10, 20, 30, 35! *(As she sits down, the track of cubes slides a little.)*

Abbie: No. We need one more, 36! *(Both children are looking only at the end and do not notice that the beginning of the track is now misaligned.)*

Julie (the teacher): *(Pointing to the misalignment of the first cube.)* Does this one count?

Abbie: Oh, it slipped. I'll hold it. *(Holds hand over the 36th cube and slides the track over to align the first cube with the edge of the paper.)* OK. So write 36 on the paper.

Julie: Show me how you got 36.

Abbie: *(Counts the cubes by ones to 36, does not make use of the tens this time, and does not align the track with the paper.)*

Julie: Do you think if we make the sign exactly this long, 36 cubes, it will match the length of the paper? Let's try cutting one and see. *(Gets some oaktag and lays the track of 36 over it.)* Do I make the mark at the edge or in the middle of the 36th cube? Does it matter?

David: In the middle, I think. It's number 36. *(Marks it in the middle.)*

Abbie: It's too big, I think. It's 35 and you gotta mark it at the end, no, between 35 and 36.

Julie: Why there?

Author's Notes

Many children do not realize that measurement is about the span of a length and that each cube is a unit of length. They focus on the quantity of the cubes in the track and on placing one end or the other at the edge of what they are measuring. It may be difficult for them to consider both edges simultaneously. You may also see some children building what looks like a picture frame around the paper and counting the cube in the corner as part of the length. For them, also, the focus is on the quantity of cubes rather than on the iteration of units to cover a distance.

repeating

By staying grounded in the context and actually cutting a strip to match the child's measurement, Julie is able to help the children realize the meaning of what they are doing.

By asking the children to reflect on where the mark gets made when measuring, Julie is asking them to reflect on what it means to measure. She is asking them to think about what the cube is: is it a unit that spans a length or is it just a quantity? Does the mark go in the middle of the cube or at the end of the unit length?

Preparing for the Math Congress

☀ Take note of the various measurement strategies and struggles you see and decide what to highlight during the math congress.

As you observe the children at work, take note of the various counting and measuring strategies and struggles you see. For example:

✦ counting tracks of cubes but not carefully aligning them to cover a span of distance

✦ building a picture frame around the paper as a way to measure both the length and width and then counting the cube in the corner as part of the measurement

✦ counting by ones consistently (a child may use the two colors, but not as a way to count groups)

✦ using the two colors to make groups and then skip-counting and counting on

✦ using the five- and/or ten-structures by making groups and then counting the number of groups, e.g., 3 tens make 30

By noting children's struggles and strategies, you can make a decision regarding which children you will have share and the problems you will raise for discussion during the congress.

▨ Tips for Structuring the Math Congress

The math congress will not be held until Day Two. Plan on structuring the congress to highlight some of the big ideas related to measurement. If you have seen children having trouble aligning the tracks or building picture frames and counting the corner cube, it is a good idea to start the discussion there. If some children have built a picture frame inside the area, and others have built it outside, you have a powerful opportunity to foster puzzlement and reflection. You might consider having both groups share and discuss why the measurements are different, and what to do with the corner cube. (If the frame was built inside, the corner cube needs to be counted twice. If the frame was built outside, the cube should not be counted at all.) Follow that with a discussion about how some of the children were using the colors to organize and keep track of the amount. Finally, if some children have used groups of five and ten, discuss how this strategy of using landmark numbers might be helpful.

Reflections on the Day

Observing and supporting children as they measured the lengths and widths of various papers gave you ample opportunity to notice how they were thinking about measurement. Did they confuse measuring with building a picture frame? What did they do with the corner cube? Did they think it was necessary to measure all four sides or did they realize that opposite sides were equal? Because only two colors of cubes were provided, some of the children may have made groups employing the use of the five- or ten-structure as a way to keep track easily. These are important observations that will provide the focus of the mathematical discussion on Day Two.

Measuring for the Art Show *repeated*

Materials Needed

Children's recording sheets from Day One

Connecting cubes (sorted to include two colors only)—one bin per pair of children

Clipboards—one per pair of children

Large chart pad and easel

Markers

Several sheets each of colored art, chart, or poster paper from Day One:
Blue:
14 cubes by 10 cubes
Purple:
22 cubes by 20 cubes
White:
35 cubes by 40 cubes
Chart paper:
46 cubes by 54 cubes
Yellow poster paper:
84 cubes by 60 cubes

Today begins with a math congress—a whole-group discussion on the strategies children used on Day One as they measured the lengths and widths of various-sized papers. The congress gives you a chance to focus on the idea of measurement as a distance of iterated units. There will also be discussion about a variety of ways to use the two colors to mark landmark numbers as a way to keep track. After the congress, children resume measuring—rechecking their results and finishing measurements they did not have time to complete on Day One. The class then creates a chart of the agreed-upon measurements.

Day Two Outline

Facilitating the Math Congress

☀ Record children's measurements on chart paper and explain that they may need to remeasure later to resolve any disagreements.

☀ Discuss the framing strategy and examine whether or not the corner cube should be counted.

☀ Highlight the use of two colors to make groups of five or ten.

Supporting the Investigation

☀ As children recheck their measurements, encourage them to try some of the strategies discussed in the math congress.

☀ Convene a whole-group meeting to resolve any lingering disagreements and record a list of final measurements.

Facilitating the Math Congress

Convene the children in the meeting area to discuss their strategies from Day One. Have them sit next to their partners with their recording sheets. Start by asking the children to share the measurements they have done thus far. Accept all answers, even wrong ones, listing them next to each other on chart paper. There will likely be disagreement. You don't need to establish right away which answer is correct. Instead, explain that when they work today they will need to check any measurements about which there are still disagreements. Go on to say that yesterday you noticed some children building something that looked like a frame around the paper (demonstrate with cubes as you talk). You wondered which cubes to count. Ask specifically about what to do with the corner cube: count it or not? (If none of the children used this framing strategy on Day One, tell them you saw it once in another class and ask them to reflect on it.)

- ☀ Record children's measurements on chart paper and explain that they may need to remeasure later to resolve any disagreements.

- ☀ Discuss the framing strategy and examine whether or not the corner cube should be counted.

- ☀ Highlight the use of two colors to make groups of five or ten.

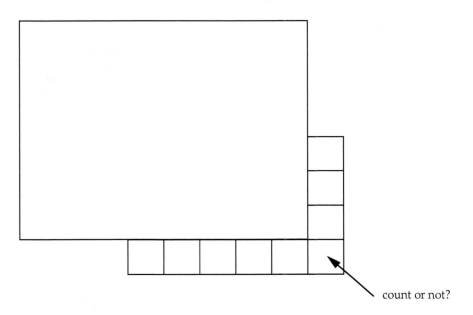

count or not?

The issue with the corner cube is that it is part of both lengths when the frame is inside. It is not part of the length of either dimension when the frame is outside. Children who are still not thinking of measurement as a total of iterated units of *distance* think that the cube should be counted. Stay in the context as a way to help children puzzle over this. Ask where the sign is going to go and have children use their hands to demonstrate the span of the sign. Turn the paper ninety degrees and ask how long the sign would be if the artwork were to be hung that way.

Author's Notes

Julie (the teacher): So it seems we have some disagreements over some of the measurements. Yesterday when I walked around I saw that a few people were measuring like this. *(Builds a frame around a piece.)* I was wondering, should we count this cube? *(Points to corner.)* Turn to the person next to you and talk about this for a minute. *(Allows time for pair talk.)* Ian, start us off. What did you and your partner decide?

Ian: Yes. Count it because you need all of those.

Julie: Who agrees with Ian? Who disagrees? Sarah, tell us why you disagree.

Sarah: I'm not sure, but I don't think the sign would go that far.

Julie: Let's make a sign and see. *(Cuts out a sign.)*

Several children: It's too long. You shouldn't count it! It has to end at the edge of the paper.

Julie: And where does it begin?

Several children: The first cube.

Julie: Where on the first cube? In the middle of it? At the end of it? At the beginning of it?

Ian: I think it has to go edge to edge. *(Holds his hands wide, showing a span.)* From the start to the end. If you do it in the middle of the cube, the sign will be a little bit too short.

Julie: So Ian thinks that it is really important to have it all. What do other people think?

Alex: Yeah. If you leave a spot, like half of a cube, it's too short.

Julie: OK. So when you go back to work today to check your work to see which of these answers is correct, make sure to carefully count just the right amount. There is a second thing I want to discuss, too. I noticed yesterday that some of you were using the two colors in ways that helped you keep track. Alex and Cassie, show us how you were measuring.

continued on next page

By accepting all the answers, but pointing out that they are different, Julie creates puzzlement. Which is right? Now there is a reason to focus on the discussion about which cubes to count and what it really means to measure a length.

By asking the children for pair talk, Julie engages all the children in considering the issue, and she pushes the children to explain what is happening.

Here the conversation does not become about what to measure, as that could be an abstraction to children. Instead, by making a sign, Julie uses the context to help children realize the meaning of what they are doing. Is the sign the right size?

repeated

The focus of the conversation here is about a big idea related to measurement: distance is measured as a series of iterated units. The complete length of each measurement unit matters!

continued from previous page

Cassie: We made groups of five and then we counted by fives: *(Alex lays out 22.)* 5, 10, 15, 20, and then 2 more.

The five- and ten-structures are now the focus.

Julie: How many of you made groups of five? *(A few hands go up.)*

Katie: We made tens and counted by tens.

Julie: How many people made groups of ten? *(A few hands go up.)*
So that is something else to think about today when you go back to finish your measuring. Is there a way the colors can be used to help you keep track?

Supporting the Investigation

Have children work with the same math partners as on Day One to finish measuring. There are many papers here to measure so have the children check to be sure of their answers. As children work, focus on their strategies. Encourage them to try some of the strategies discussed in the math congress. After the children have had sufficient time to work, bring them back to the meeting area and list their answers on chart paper. If there is still disagreement over some of the measurements, discuss the disagreements and remeasure together. Ensure that the measurements in the list are agreed upon because they will be used on Day Three to create a blueprint (which over the course of this unit will become a number line):

☀ As children recheck their measurements, encourage them to try some of the strategies discussed in the math congress.

☀ Convene a whole-group meeting to resolve any lingering disagreements and record a list of final measurements.

+ Blue: 14 cubes by 10 cubes

+ Purple: 22 cubes by 20 cubes

+ White: 35 cubes by 40 cubes

+ Chart paper: 46 cubes by 54 cubes

+ Yellow poster paper: 84 cubes by 60 cubes

Assessment Tips

As the children go off to resume their measuring, jot down on sticky notes your recollections of important things children said during the congress. Now, as you observe the children at work, note if their strategies have changed. Do they make use of fives and tens, instead of counting by ones? Are they measuring more carefully? It is helpful to record these observations as well. Later, you can place your notes on children's recording sheets to be included in their portfolios.

Differentiating Instruction

By allowing children to mathematize this situation in their own ways, you can be assured that you are differentiating appropriately. As you support them as they measure, continue to note where they need help. Use the context to help children realize the meaning of what they are doing. Talk about the signs. Remind children that they might like to use the two colors to help them keep track. For those children you want to challenge, ask them to use various-sized groups. For example, if they know a measurement is 3 tens and 5 cubes long, can they figure out how many groups of five that will be?

Reflections on the Day

Today children were encouraged to really think about what it means to measure a length. Several ideas and strategies were discussed in the math congress and then children resumed their work of measuring and rechecking previous results. At the end of the day, the class reached consensus on the measurements and posted a chart with the results.

Building the Blueprint

The day begins with a minilesson designed to support children's ability, over time, to add groups of ten to numbers with ease. Place value patterns appear and children discuss the reasons for those patterns. The work of building a blueprint with the results of their measuring then begins. A string of cubes with alternating groups of five in two colors is provided as a support to children as they consider where to place the marks on the blueprint.

Day Three Outline

Minilesson: Around the Circle

* Have children add ten to various numbers and record the results.

* Discuss the place value pattern in the results and examine why it is happening.

Developing the Context

* Work with the children to create a blueprint of their measurements using connecting cubes and adding machine paper.

* Mark the measurements on the blueprint.

Materials Needed

Roll of adding machine paper, about three inches wide

Chart with list of measurements from Day Two

Large chart pad and easel

Markers

Pointer or yardstick

A string of 100 connecting cubes, in two colors, arranged in alternating groups of five cubes of each color.

Before class you should hang this across the chalkboard, out of children's reach. You'll need room directly beneath the cubes to hang a strip of adding machine paper, and room under that to record measurements (see page 24).

Minilesson: Around the Circle (10–15 minutes)

☀ Have children add ten to various numbers and record the results.

☀ Discuss the place value pattern in the results and examine why it is happening.

Gather the children in the meeting area and have them sit in a circle. Have one child choose a number between 1 and 9. Write it on top of a large sheet of chart paper. Go around the circle having each child add 10. Record the results on the chart. For example, if a child chooses 3, you would be recording 13, 23, 33, 43, 53, etc. Discuss the pattern (the number of tens goes up by one each time, while the number of units stays the same). Ask, "Will this always happen?" Try a few more numbers such as 7 or 8, adding 10 repeatedly, as before. Ask why they think the pattern is happening.

Developing the Context

☀ Work with the children to create a blueprint of their measurements using connecting cubes and adding machine paper.

☀ Mark the measurements on the blueprint.

Tell children that today you will be making a blueprint just like in the story *Measuring for the Art Show.* Explain that you will be putting their measurements onto a strip of adding machine paper. A friend of yours will then use that as a blueprint—a pattern—to cut out the signs.

Have the chart of measurements from Day Two available for reference. Begin by asking a child to tell you the measurement of the short side of the blue paper (10 cubes). Ask where to mark the 10 on the paper. (You might find it helpful to use a pointer or a yardstick. The purpose of hanging the cubes high is to stop children from counting by ones and to challenge them to use the five-structure.) Ask for different ways to figure out where the 10 is, such as adding 2 fives or counting. Ask, "Do I mark at the edge of the cube? On the cube? Where?" These questions revisit the discussion from the congress on Day Two to ensure that children continue to think about measuring as a length of iterated units. Make a line with a marker to indicate the 10 and write 10 on the chalkboard underneath.

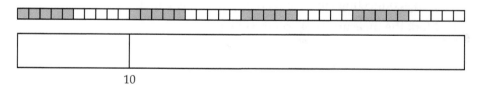

10

Continue in this fashion, marking the other numbers: 14, 20, 22, 35, 40, 46, 54, 60, and 84, encouraging the children to use the five- and ten-structures to help them decide where the marks go.

Once the measurements are up, tell the children that you have another type of paper at home that might be nice for the art show as well. It measures 72 cubes long. Ask them where they think this one might go. Seek alternate strategies and discuss them.

Inside One Classroom

Sean: I think it is in the middle between 84 and 60. 'Cause if you go up 10 from 60, that's 70, and if you go 10 back from 84, that's 74, so 72 . . . it's in the middle.

Julie (the teacher): Wow. Who understands what Sean said? Who can put his idea in your own words? *(Only two hands go up.)* Sean, tell us again.

Sean : I'll show you. *(Comes up and gets the pointer.)* See, if you go back from 84, that's 74.

Julie: How many did you go back?

Sean : Ten.

Julie: Do we agree? *(Some kids are counting.)*

Sean : And then from 60 to 70 is 10. So 72 is in the middle, there.

Julie: Turn to the person you are next to and talk about that. *(Allow time for pair talk.)* Janet?

Janet: He is right. Because I did it as 7 tens. That's 70 and 2 more. It is right there.

Author's Notes

By asking for paraphrasing, Julie implies that it is important to listen to others and to try to understand their ideas. This act alone goes a long way in establishing a mathematical community. It also provides Julie with a quick check to see how many children understand. When only a few hands go up, Julie invites Sean to explain again.

Julie does not acknowledge the answer as correct but invites the community to consider if it works.

Pair talk further pushes the children to reflect on the mathematics and to decide for themselves if the strategy works.

Reflections on the Day

Today's minilesson encouraged children to use place value patterns to take leaps of ten. Using the five-structure provided by alternating groups of two colors of cubes further encouraged children to make use of landmark numbers. As the blueprint was developed, children were supported to think about number space—a measurement line with numbers in relation to each other on it. This emerging model will soon become an open number line.

DAY FOUR
Measuring with Strips of Ten

Materials Needed

Various new sets of paper (see Differentiating Instruction, page 28)

Strips of ten (Appendix C)

Two versions of the strips of ten are provided. You will want to choose the version that corresponds to the size of the connecting cubes you have been using. Before class, these strips should be cut out and taped together to make one long measuring strip for class use. Be sure the strip is long enough to encompass all the measurements for the new sets of paper.

Strips of ten (Appendix C) —one set per child

Student recording sheet for the strips of ten investigation (Appendix D)—two sheets per pair of children

Tape—for each child

Scissors—one pair per child

Large chart pad and easel

Markers

A minilesson, similar to Day Three, reminds children of the place value pattern when adding groups of ten. Today, though, you cross over the 100 mark, encouraging children to look for complete groups of ten—for example, 129 as 12 tens and 9 units, rather than as just 1 hundred, 2 tens, and 9 units. As you develop the context for the next investigation, a new measurement tool, strips of ten, is introduced. After creating this new tool, children use it to measure a new set of papers.

Day Four Outline

Minilesson: Around the Circle

☀ Have children add ten to various numbers and record the results.

☀ Discuss how the place value pattern continues when you pass 100.

Developing the Context

☀ Introduce the paper ten-strip measuring tool.

Supporting the Investigation

☀ Have children make their own measuring strips by cutting out strips of ten and taping them together.

☀ Confer with children as they measure more papers with their new ten-strip tools.

Preparing for the Math Congress

☀ Take note of the children who are still counting by ones.

Minilesson: Around the Circle (10–15 minutes)

This is a repeat of the minilesson on Day Three, but with different numbers. Gather the children in the meeting area and have them sit in a circle. Have one child choose a number between 1 and 9. Write it on top of a large sheet of chart paper. Go around the circle having each child add 10. Record the results on the chart. For example, if a child chooses 9, you would be recording 19, 29, 39, 49, 59, etc. Discuss how the pattern continues when you go past 100: 99, 109, 119, 129, etc. Help the children notice that the pattern from Day Three is continuing (the number of tens goes up by one each time, while the number of units stays the same). Do not focus on the columns by asking "How many hundreds, how many tens?" Thinking of 119 as just 1 hundred, 1 ten, and 9 units obscures the increasing tens pattern! Establish that 1 hundred has 10 tens, so 1 hundred and 1 ten makes 11 tens. Develop the idea of equivalence, that 119 can be thought of as 11 tens and 9 units, and also as 1 hundred, 1 ten, and 9 units.

- ☀ Have children add ten to various numbers and record the results.

- ☀ Discuss how the place value pattern continues when you pass 100.

Developing the Context

Explain that you took the blueprint home last night and gave it to your friend who is going to cut out the signs. But on the way to school today you remembered a few more types of paper for which you'll need signs. Then you had a brilliant idea. You thought that since so many of the children were using fives and tens as they were building the blueprint yesterday, why not use a paper ten-strip that has two colors, instead of the cubes? These strips could be used to measure things as needed all year and would be much easier to work with than all those cubes!

Demonstrate measuring the length of a large piece of paper with the class measuring strip that you made from the strips of ten in Appendix C.

- ☀ Introduce the paper ten-strip measuring tool.

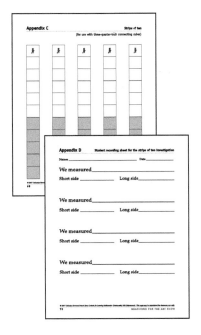

Supporting the Investigation

Distribute two sheets of ten-strips (Appendix C) to each child and have the children go to tables to make their own measuring strips by cutting out the strips of ten and taping them together. Then assign partners and provide each pair with a recording sheet (Appendix D). Working with their partners, the children should measure the new papers, check with their partners for agreement, and then note their measurements on the recording sheet.

If children do not tape carefully, they may have small gaps in their strips and their measurements will differ. Don't try to fix the measurements or the strips! Work with the young mathematicians! This is a prime "teaching moment." Maximize it. Bring the children together to discuss why these gaps might matter or confer with them as they work. Some children still may not have constructed the idea that measurement is about covering a length. This is a perfect moment to revisit this idea. If, after this discussion, children are still struggling to tape without gaps, you can then help because they now recognize the mathematical need for it.

- ☀ Have children make their own measuring strips by cutting out strips of ten and taping them together.

- ☀ Confer with children as they measure more papers with their new ten-strip tools.

Differentiating Instruction

Before you cut the papers for this activity, think about how you might want to differentiate instruction. You might want to challenge some children with larger papers, using lengths that are greater than 100. Other children might benefit from measuring smaller sizes. You can then distribute the new papers accordingly.

■ Assessment Tips

As the children begin to measure, note whether their strategies have changed. Do they make use of fives and tens, instead of counting by ones? Are they measuring more carefully? It is helpful to jot down your observations on sticky notes. Later, you can place these on children's recording sheets to be included in their portfolios.

Preparing for the Math Congress

☀ Take note of the children who are still counting by ones.

As you walk around and confer with children, note the children who are still struggling to use the ten-strips, i.e., they are measuring with the strips but still counting by ones. In the congress on Day Five you will want to ensure that they are involved and that you are supporting them to make use of the five- and ten- structures.

Have children fold up the new measuring tool, at the decades where they taped, like an accordion. Have them place the measuring strips and their recording sheets in their work folders.

Reflections on the Day

During the minilesson today, children were encouraged to see the increasing patterns of tens even when crossing the 100 mark. Understanding why this pattern occurs helped them to understand more deeply our place value system. This idea will become the basis of an important strategy for double-digit mental arithmetic, where one number is kept whole and leaps of ten and landmark numbers are used. As children used strips of ten to make a new measuring tool, they were further supported to make use of the five- and ten-structures.

Measuring with Strips of Ten

The major part of the math workshop today is devoted to a math congress. During the congress, children discuss where to place marks on the class measuring strip. They are given time to check out any discrepant answers and to ensure that ultimately everyone agrees with the results. Measurements are also recorded on a chart to support the development of an important big idea related to measurement: measurements can be different when different units are used, but the results are equivalent. The original set of papers from Days One and Two is also remeasured with the new class measuring strip and those results are added to the chart.

Day Five Outline

Facilitating the Math Congress

☀ Have the children share their measurements from Day Four and add them to the class measuring strip.

☀ List the measurements in a chart and discuss the place value pattern that develops. Ask children if they think the pattern will continue.

☀ Have children remeasure the papers from Days One and Two, this time using their ten-strip tool, and add those measurements to the chart.

Materials Needed

Class measuring strip from Day Four

Children's recording sheets and individual measuring strips from Day Four

Large chart pad and easel

Markers

Tape

Sets of paper from Day One:
Blue:
14 cubes by 10 cubes
Purple:
22 cubes by 20 cubes
White:
35 cubes by 40 cubes
Chart paper:
46 cubes by 54 cubes
Yellow poster paper:
84 cubes by 60 cubes

Facilitating the Math Congress

☀ Have the children share their measurements from Day Four and add them to the class measuring strip.

☀ List the measurements in a chart and discuss the place value pattern that develops. Ask children if they think the pattern will continue.

☀ Have children remeasure the papers from Days One and Two, this time using their ten-strip tool, and add those measurements to the chart.

Convene the children in the meeting area to discuss their measurements from Day Four. Have them sit next to their partners with their recording sheets. Tape the class measuring strip across the chalkboard. Next to the chalkboard have a large piece of chart paper. Ask for the measurements, one at a time. Discuss with the group where each measurement would be on the strip. For example, if a piece was 3 ten-strips long plus 2 (32 cubes), mark it as follows:

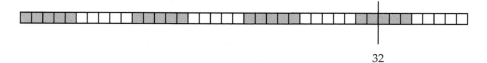

32

On the chart make three columns and fill in the data like this:

Paper	Measurement	Total
lined chart paper	3 ten-strips, plus 2	32

The purpose of the chart is to provide children with a representation of the results of the overall number, both in units and in groups of ten and units, for example 32 as also 3 ten-strips plus 2. As you fill in the chart, it is highly likely that several children will notice the place value pattern. Ask if they think this pattern will continue. Enjoy their surprise and excitement when it does. If no one notices the pattern, you can point it out. For example, you might comment, "Isn't that interesting. Look at what I just noticed! There is a pattern. I wonder if this will continue."

Once all the new measurements have been marked on both the measuring strip and the chart, and some discussion has occurred on the place value pattern, have the children return to the pieces of paper they measured on Days One and Two and remeasure them with their individual measuring strips. Add these measurements to the chart. Save this chart, as you will use it on Day Six.

Reflections on the Day

Today children developed a chart to compare the results of measuring with two different tools. Place value patterns appeared on the chart and children were invited to consider how and why the pattern was happening: for example, 3 tens plus 2 was the result with the ten-strips and 32 was the result with cubes.

Exploring Addition

Materials Needed

Class measuring strip hung across the chalkboard (this strip now needs to be at least 11 ten-strips long)

Chart with list of measurements from Day Five

Student recording sheet for the two pieces investigation (Appendix E)—one per pair of children

Children's measuring strips from Day Five

Large chart pad and easel

Markers

Sets of paper from Day One:
Blue:
14 cubes by 10 cubes
Purple:
22 cubes by 20 cubes
White:
35 cubes by 40 cubes
Chart paper:
46 cubes by 54 cubes

Before class, tape two sheets of blue paper together to make a sheet 20 cubes by 14 cubes. Do not overlap the edges when taping.

Double-digit addition becomes the focus in this second week. Today's minilesson reviews taking leaps of ten, but in the context of measurement. The minilesson paves the way for the introduction of an addition context: measuring the total length of art pieces that are created on *two* sheets of paper put together. This context encourages children to make use of landmarks and to take leaps of ten as they add. In a subsequent math congress they will share their addition strategies, which will then be recorded on the class measuring strip.

Day Six Outline

Minilesson: Around the Circle, with Measurements

☀ Have children add ten to the measurements from the chart created on Day Five and discuss the place value pattern in the results.

Developing the Context

☀ Explain how new signs are needed for larger pieces of art.

☀ Use the class measuring strip to record some of these new measurements and create a chart to keep track of them.

☀ Represent the addition as jumps on the measuring strip.

Supporting the Investigation

☀ Note children's strategies as they work on Appendix E, using the measurement strips as a tool.

Preparing for the Math Congress

☀ As children make posters of their work, plan for a math congress discussion that will highlight important computation strategies for addition.

Facilitating the Math Congress

☀ Represent children's strategies as jumps on the class measuring strip.

☀ Highlight the use of landmark numbers as a helpful strategy.

Minilesson: Around the Circle, with Measurements
(10–15 minutes)

Gather the children in the meeting area and have them sit in a circle. Have one child choose one of the measurements from the chart, such as 22. Write it on top of a large sheet of chart paper. Go around the circle having each child add 10. Record the results on the chart. For example, if a child chooses 22, you would be recording 32, 42, 52, 62, etc. Continue with a different measurement. Discuss the pattern.

☀ Have children add ten to the measurements from the chart created on Day Five and discuss the place value pattern in the results.

Developing the Context

Tell the children that you realized that it might be helpful to tape two papers together, because sometimes artists want to make really large pieces of art. Demonstrate with two sheets of the blue paper. Explain that new signs now have to be cut for these situations.

☀ Explain how new signs are needed for larger pieces of art.

☀ Use the class measuring strip to record some of these new measurements and create a chart to keep track of them.

☀ Represent the addition as jumps on the measuring strip.

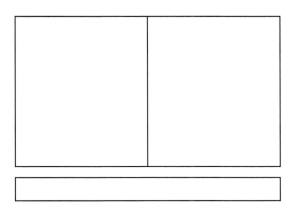

Above the measuring strip draw the jumps of 10 to represent the two groups of 10:

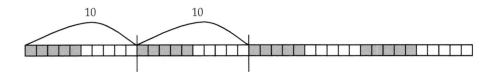

Start a new chart labeled "Two Pieces Together." Fill in the chart like this:

Paper	Measurement	Total
2 blue, short side	10 + 10	20
2 blue, long side	14 + 14	

It is important to draw the leaps above the measuring strip. Although the chart will have a representation of the result of the addition—the answer—the leaps represent the action to derive the answer. Here the measuring strip is beginning to emerge as a number line to record addition strategies. Over time it will become a tool to think with.

Supporting the Investigation

Appendix E	Student recording sheet for the two pieces investigation	
Paper	Measurement	Total
2 blue, short side	10 + 10	20
2 blue, long side	14 + 14	
2 purple, short side	20 + 20	
2 purple, long side	22 + 22	
2 white, short side	35 + 35	
2 white, long side	40 + 40	
2 chart paper, short side	46 + 46	
2 chart paper, long side	54 + 54	

Assign math partners and provide each pair with a recording sheet (Appendix E). Have the children move to tables to complete the sheet.

As you observe and confer, take note of which children are reliant on their measuring strip and still need to count by ones, and which are making use of the strategies of adding tens that you have been working on in the minilessons. Remind the children of the minilesson Around the Circle, and encourage them to try adding tens. Remind them of the pattern on the measuring chart from Day Five, i.e., how 32 was 3 ten-strips, plus 2. Suggest that they make the addition friendly either by using some of the extras to get to a full ten-strip and then adding tens or by adding tens first, then the extras. For example, 46 + 46 might be solved as 46 + 4 + 10 + 10 + 10 + 10 + 2, as 40 + 40 + 6 + 6, or as 46 + 40 + 4 + 2, etc. Keeping one number whole and taking leaps of ten, moving to a landmark decade, and splitting are important strategies for mental arithmetic.

Differentiating Instruction

As you observe the children at work, take note of the different strategies they are using. For children who are struggling to count, help them use the measuring strip as a manipulative and encourage them either to count on with it or to make leaps to landmark numbers, using the five- or ten-structure. Encourage those who are already taking leaps to landmark numbers to take even bigger leaps.

Preparing for the Math Congress

Have children make posters of a couple of the strategies they want to share. As they do so, think about how you will structure the math congress discussion so as to focus on computation strategies for addition.

▨ Tips for Structuring the Math Congress

Consider starting the math congress with a child who is still counting on by ones. Then scaffold the discussion in a way that supports the development of more efficient strategies for addition—for example, by highlighting the work of children who are taking leaps of ten and using landmarks.

Facilitating the Math Congress

Convene the children in the meeting area to discuss some of the strategies they used. As the children share, record their strategies on the class measuring strip. This representation of the action of the addition serves as an image for discussion of the various strategies. Using the number line model this way is stage two in the development of modeling (see description on pages 8–9).

The figure below is a representation of 35 + 35 if a child's strategy was to take leaps of ten and add the remainder of five at the end. Encourage a discussion on how long it takes to count by ones and how it is helpful to use friendly numbers, like tens.

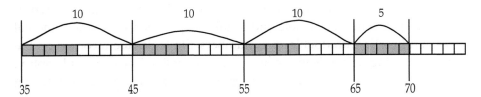

☀ Represent children's strategies as jumps on the class measuring strip.

☀ Highlight the use of landmark numbers as a helpful strategy.

▣ Assessment Tips

After the math congress, jot down on sticky notes your observations regarding the big ideas you heard individual children express clearly and the strategies they used. Place these on the child's recording sheet along with any other anecdotal notes and put in the child's portfolio. You may also want to photocopy the landscape of learning graphic (page 11) and, for each student, shade in the landmarks as you find evidence in their work. Note the children you are not sure of, for whom you have no evidence. Over the next few days you will want to be sure to observe them at work.

Reflections on the Day

Today, children were introduced to double-digit addition and encouraged to use several strategies, such as treating one number as a whole and taking leaps of ten, using landmarks, and decomposing using partial sums. These strategies became the focus of a subsequent math congress. The strategies were modeled on the class measuring strip as leaps on a number line.

Developing Addition Strategies

Materials Needed

Class measuring strip hung across the chalkboard

Leapfrog game cards (Appendix F)—one set per pair of children

Leapfrog game board (Appendix G)—one per child

Number cubes—two per pair of children

Leapfrog game pieces (plastic frogs or other game pieces that can be moved around the board)—one per child

Markers

This day begins with a minilesson designed to encourage children to keep one number whole and to take leaps of ten for efficient mental arithmetic with double-digit numbers. Strategies are recorded on the class measuring strip as leaps on an open number line. The game of Leapfrog is then introduced to encourage and reinforce the addition strategy of taking leaps of ten.

Day Seven Outline

Minilesson: An Addition String

☀ Work on a string of related problems designed to support children in taking leaps of ten.

☀ Represent children's strategies as jumps on the class measuring strip.

Developing the Context

☀ Model how to play Leapfrog.

Supporting the Investigation

☀ Note children's addition strategies as they play the game, and support them in using place value when adding ten.

Minilesson: An Addition String (10–15 minutes)

This mental math minilesson uses a string of related problems designed to encourage children to keep one number whole and take leaps of ten. Do one problem at a time and record children's strategies on the class measuring strip, inviting other children to comment on the representations.

As you progress through the string and notice children beginning to make use of the tens, discuss why this strategy is helpful. If the class agrees that it is a useful strategy for addition, you might want to make a sign for it and post it near the meeting area. Over time you will have several signs of "Helpful Addition Strategies" posted on a strategy wall.

☀ Work on a string of related problems designed to support children in taking leaps of ten.

☀ Represent children's strategies as jumps on the class measuring strip.

String of related problems:

26 + 10

26 + 12

26 + 22

44 + 30

44 + 39

57 + 39

Behind the Numbers

Since the string is designed to encourage children to keep one number whole and to take leaps of ten, the first problem lays the terrain for this strategy. The second problem is just 2 more and can be added right onto the representation of the first. The third problem requires another jump of 10. The fourth problem lays the terrain for the fifth, which is just 9 more. This fifth problem also provides an opening for children to add 40 and subtract 1. The last problem has no helper problem provided. Here children have to think about how to make the problem friendly.

Inside One Classroom

A Portion of the Minilesson

Julie (the teacher): Here's our first warm-up problem: 26 + 10. Thumbs-up when you have an answer. Michael?

Michael: 36. I just know. I used the pattern of adding ten.
(Referring to past minilessons, Around the Circle.)

Julie: *(Draws the following representation of Michael's strategy.)*

Does everyone agree with Michael? *(No disagreement is apparent.)* OK. Let's go to the next one: 26 + 12. Emmy?
continued on next page

Author's Notes

Since Michael did not count on but just added on a group of ten, Julie represents it as a leap of ten. If a child had counted, Julie would have needed to represent ten little jumps.

continued from previous page

Emmy: I did a jump of two more onto the last problem.

Julie: Let's see what that looks like on the strip.
(She records the jumps in a different color.)

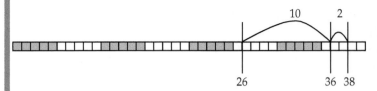

By building on the other representation, Julie supports children to consider how the problems are related.

Julie: What do you think? Does Emmy's way work? Saves a lot of counting, doesn't it, if we think of 12 as 10 and 2? OK, let's go on to the next problem: 26 + 22. Show me with your thumb when you are ready. *(Allows several minutes of think time.)* Susie?

Susie: It's 48, I think. I did 20 + 20 + 8.

Julie: Nice. You used the friendly number of 20 and added them. Let me record your strategy.

By providing long moments of think time, Julie gives the children ample opportunity to work through their strategies. This also communicates the message that thinking is valued. By using a signal like "thumbs-up when ready," Julie can gauge when to start discussion.

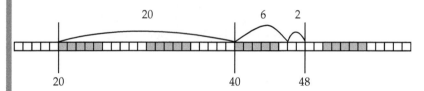

Did anybody do it a different way? Did anyone do what Emmy did last time and use the problem before?

Alternative strategies are valued and explored.

Michael: I did. I just added on 10 more. So 38 . . . then 48.

Julie: Nice. It is really helpful to keep one number whole, isn't it? And just add on. Here's the next one: 44 + 30. Remember how we did all the patterns in Around the Circle? See if that idea would be helpful here.

Abbie: It is! It's just 54, 64 . . . 74.

Julie: How many of you agree with Abbie? Let's think about this as we continue with our string. If we agree at the end, we can make a sign and post it on our "Helpful Strategies for Addition" wall.

An invitation to consider a strategy is given, but the use of it is not required. It is left to the young mathematicians to decide if it can be helpful or not.

Developing the Context

Have the children sit in a circle in the meeting area. Play a game of Leapfrog with one child as a way to introduce the game to the class and model for them how it is played.

☀ Model how to play Leapfrog.

▧ Object of the Game

The purpose of the game is to support the development of the addition strategy of keeping one number whole and taking leaps of ten.

▧ Directions for Playing Leapfrog

Children play the game in pairs and take turns rolling the number cubes. The roll of the cubes determines the number of steps to move.

For example, if Player One rolls a 3 and a 4, the frog game piece jumps 7 spaces and Player One writes 7 in the corresponding box on the game board (Appendix G). Player One then turns over a card from the deck of Leapfrog cards (Appendix F). The card indicates how many leaps of ten to take. For example, if the card says "Leap 2 tens," Player One jumps to 17 and writes 17 in the box, then jumps to 27 and records 27.

Now it is Player Two's turn. Player Two rolls the number cubes, takes a card, and marks his game board accordingly.

Player One then rolls again, takes a card, and marks her game board. For example, if she rolls a 4 and a 2 and the card says "Leap 1 ten," she moves the frog piece to 33 (i.e., 27 + 6) and then to 43, or from 27 to 37 and then 6 more to 43.

Play continues in this way until both frogs reach the end of their tracks.

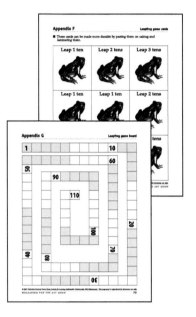

Supporting the Investigation

Children are assigned math partners and go to tables to play the game. Each child has a game board and a frog game piece. Each pair of children also has two number cubes and a deck of Leapfrog cards. As children play the game, watch a few groups. Notice the strategies they are using. Can they take a jump of ten all at once and make use of the place value pattern, or do they still need to count on by ones?

☀ Note children's addition strategies as they play the game and support them in using place value when adding ten.

▧ Assessment Tips

As you support children as they play the game, note which children need to count. Also note their counting strategies, such as whether they are counting each dot on the cube or whether they can subitize the amount and add without needing to count. Note if they use the place value pattern when adding ten or if they are still counting by ones. It is helpful to jot down your observations on sticky notes. Later, you can place these on children's recording sheets to be included in their portfolios.

Reflections on the Day

Today children participated in a minilesson designed to encourage the addition strategy of keeping one number whole and taking leaps of ten. This strategy was further reinforced with the game of Leapfrog. As children played the game, you had the opportunity to notice which of them can use place value patterns to make leaps of ten all at once and which still need to count on by ones when they are adding ten.

Developing
Addition Strategies

Today's minilesson continues to encourage children to explore how it is easier to use leaps of ten, but it extends that strategy to include decomposing to get to a landmark number. The open number line is introduced in place of the measuring strip. Children are then taught another version of the Leapfrog game, called Fly Capture. This version encourages moving to landmark numbers when adding.

Day Eight Outline

Minilesson: An Addition String

☀ Work on a string of related problems designed to support the use of decomposing to get to a landmark number.

☀ Record children's strategies on an open number line.

Developing the Context

☀ Model how to play Fly Capture.

Supporting the Investigation

☀ Note children's strategies as they play the game and encourage the use of landmark numbers.

Materials Needed

Leapfrog game cards (from Day Seven)—one set per pair of children

Leapfrog game board (Appendix G)—one per child

Number cubes—two per pair of children

Leapfrog game pieces—one per child

Counters (such as buttons or cubes)—ten per child

Markers

Minilesson: An Addition String (10–15 minutes)

☀ Work on a string of related problems designed to support the use of decomposing to get to a landmark number.

☀ Record children's strategies on an open number line.

This mental math minilesson uses a string of related problems to encourage children to continue to explore the addition strategy of using leaps of ten, but it extends that strategy to include decomposing an addend to get to a landmark number. As before, do one problem at a time. This time record children's strategies on the open number line, explaining that they have gotten so good at taking leaps you think you will just draw a line instead of using the measuring strip.

In contrast to a number line with counting numbers written below, an "open" number line is just an empty line used to record children's addition (and later subtraction) strategies. Only the numbers children use are recorded, and the addition is recorded as leaps, or jumps. For example, if a child's strategy for adding 59 + 11 is to keep 59 whole and decompose the 11, moving to a landmark number of 60—59 + 1 + 10—it can be recorded like this:

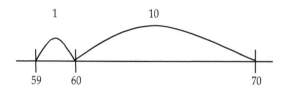

Behind the Numbers

Since the string is designed to encourage keeping one number whole and decomposing the other addend to get to a landmark number, the first problem is used to lay the terrain. The second problem is just 10 more than the first. The third problem has no prior scaffold, but 50 is a strong landmark for children and they may think to use the 2 (from the 12) to get there. After children share their strategies for the third problem, if none have decomposed to get to 50, you might wonder aloud if that strategy would have worked and show it. The fourth problem allows children to test the strategy out again. The fifth and sixth are paired to continue supporting the strategy, although this time the 6—a single-digit number—has to be decomposed. The last problem in the string requires children to make their own equivalent problem, such as 60 + 30 + 2 or 60 + 32.

If you notice children beginning to make use of landmark numbers as you progress through the string, invite a discussion on how helpful it might be to do that. If the class agrees that this is indeed a helpful strategy, you might want to make a sign for it and add it to your wall of "Helpful Addition Strategies."

String of related problems:

59 + 1

59 + 11

48 + 12

58 + 22

38 + 6

38 + 26

59 + 33

Assessment Tips

Note the strategies children are using during this and other minilessons. Remember to pay particular attention to the children for whom you do not yet have evidence. As the unit progresses, also pay particular attention to children's growth and development and track their progress on the landscape graphic.

Developing the Context

Bring the children to the meeting area and have them sit in a circle. Play Fly Capture with one child as a way to introduce the game to the class and model how it is played.

☀ Model how to play Fly Capture.

Object of the Game

The purpose of this game is to encourage children to move to landmark numbers when adding.

Directions for Playing Fly Capture

Children play the game in pairs and take turns rolling the number cubes and taking a card, just as they did with Leapfrog. The roll determines the number of steps to move and the card determines the number of jumps. The players can use the number cubes and the cards in any order.

The difference in this variation is that players want to land on as many of the decade landmarks as possible. Each time players land on 10, 20, 30, etc., they capture a "fly." (Counters such as buttons or cubes can be used to represent the flies.) The intent is to capture as many flies as possible as the frogs move around the track on the game board. For example, Player One begins the game by taking a "Leap 2 tens" card and rolling a 2 and a 4 with the number cubes. Player One could move 6 first and then take two jumps of ten. But, if he uses the card first (before using the sum of the numbers on the number cubes), his frog lands on 10 and 20, thereby capturing two flies, before moving to 26. On his next turn, Player One rolls a 3 and a 5 and picks a "Leap 1 ten" card. Four from the eight rolled can be used to get the frog from 26 to 30 (thereby capturing another fly), the card can be used to get to 40 (capturing another fly), and then the remaining four from the roll is used to get the frog to 44.

Play continues as in Leapfrog, with all landings recorded, until the frogs reach the end of their tracks. Play is collaborative, with players helping each other to capture as many flies as possible. At the end, players record the total number of flies captured.

Supporting the Investigation

※ Note children's strategies as they play the game and encourage the use of landmark numbers.

Children are assigned math partners and go to tables to play the game. Each pair of children has a deck of Leapfrog cards and two number cubes. Each child has a game board and a frog game piece.

▩ Assessment Tips

Note the strategies children are using as they play the game. Is it difficult or easy for them to decompose and move to a landmark? Remember to pay particular attention to the children for whom you do not yet have enough evidence. As the unit progresses, also pay particular attention to the growth and development of the children and record their pathways on the landscape graphic.

Differentiating Instruction

Moving to the nearest landmark is easy only if a child has memorized the combinations that make ten. Children who do not know these combinations can benefit from using the arithmetic rack and/or from playing games like Rack Ten, Rolling for Tens, and Capture Ten. See the units *The Double-Decker Bus* and *Games for Early Number Sense* for more information.

Reflections on the Day

The minilesson today encouraged children to move to landmark numbers as an addition strategy for mental arithmetic. Fly Capture supported the development of this strategy. The activities have given you an opportunity to notice which children use this strategy easily and which children are still struggling.

Developing Addition Strategies

The day begins with a minilesson designed to support the addition strategy of decomposing to make equivalent but friendlier problems—for example, turning 38 + 42 into 40 + 40. Children then work on pages for a class book about measuring for their own art show—they describe the addition strategies they have learned as they worked with the investigations, games, and minilessons in this unit. Their work on the class book will be used to assess their strategies for addition and their development along the landscape of learning.

Day Nine Outline

Minilesson: An Addition String

☀ Work on a string of related problems designed to support children to use decomposing to get to a landmark number.

☀ Record children's strategies on an open number line.

Developing the Context

☀ Invite the class to create their own big book to document their work of the past two weeks.

Supporting the Investigation

☀ Take note of children's strategies as they work on the problems in Appendix H.

Materials Needed

Student recording sheets for addition strategies (Appendix H)—one set per child

Minilesson: An Addition String (10–15 minutes)

☀ Work on a string of related problems designed to support children to use decomposing to get to a landmark number.

☀ Record children's strategies on an open number line.

This mental math minilesson uses a string of related problems that encourages children to continue decomposing to make problems friendlier. As before, do one problem at a time and record children's strategies on the open number line, inviting other children to comment on the representations and to share alternative strategies. If you notice children beginning to make use of the related problems as you progress through the string, invite a discussion on how helpful it might be to do that. Suggest that they try to make problems into friendlier ones, as mathematicians do, and make signs of the important strategies to add to your "Helpful Addition Strategies" wall.

Behind the Numbers

The first several problems in this string are all related in ways that will support and encourage children to think about decomposing to make problems friendlier. The first six problems in the string are clustered into pairs that have the same answer. If children have not noticed the relationships after the sixth problem, point out that several of the answers are the same and ask which is the easiest to do. Once children realize that the answers are the same, discuss why that is happening. Represent the problems on the number line and discuss how the problems involve sliding up and down the number line, but that the total stays the same. Here you are beginning to use the number line as a tool to think with. Once the compensation strategy is understood, encourage children to use it to make the last two problems friendlier. For example, 98 + 42 becomes an easy problem to solve when children realize it is equivalent to 100 + 40.

String of related problems:

58 + 22

60 + 20

30 + 50

28 + 52

32 + 48

33 + 47

———————

98 + 42

97 + 34

Developing the Context

☀ Invite that the class to create their own big book to document their work of the past two weeks.

Once rich discussion has occurred on several addition strategies, tell the children that you will be putting together a class big book—a sequel to *Measuring for the Art Show*. This book will document the story of what they did, all the measurements they took, their work with the ten-strips and the data, and their art show. Today they will complete a few of the pages (see Appendix H) by solving several addition problems and explaining the strategies they have learned as they progressed through this unit.

The book should contain all the data you used, the findings of the children, the big ideas discussed about measurement and addition, and the clever strategies the class constructed. The book also gives children a "sociohistorical" view of the work—a developmental perspective—to revisit and reflect on even after the unit has ended. They will enjoy reflecting on their early ideas, the conjectures, the moments of despair and puzzlement, and the big ah-ha moments as the mathematics emerged in their community.

Supporting the Investigation

Pass out a set of recording sheets (Appendix H) to each child. As you observe the children at work, note the strategies they write about and celebrate their accomplishments with them.

Take note of children's strategies as they work on the problems in Appendix H.

Appendix H
Student recording sheet for addition strategies
38 + 10 =
My strategy was
49 + 51 =
My strategy was

Assessment Tips

These recording sheets are designed as an individual assessment. Work space is provided for each of the problems so you can see the strategies each child uses. Note the strategies, paying particular attention to the growth and development of the children. Color in the landmarks on the landscape of learning graphic to record where each child is on the journey. Make copies of the recording sheets and place them in the children's portfolios.

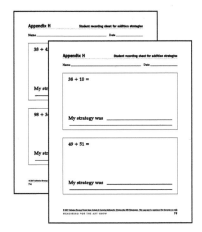

Sample Children's Work

Figure 1 shows a child using a strategy of keeping one addend whole and decomposing the other to get to a landmark (in this case 100). Figure 2 shows a compensation strategy to make doubles. Figure 3 is representative of a splitting strategy; both numbers are decomposed into partial sums. Although this strategy shows some number sense, a much more efficient strategy here would have been to compensate and make doubles (50 + 50). Figure 4 is illustrative of a child who does not yet employ place value, but counts on.

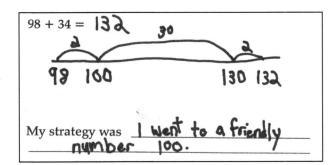

98 + 34 = 132
2
30
2
98 100
130 132
My strategy was I went to a friendly number 100.

Figure 1

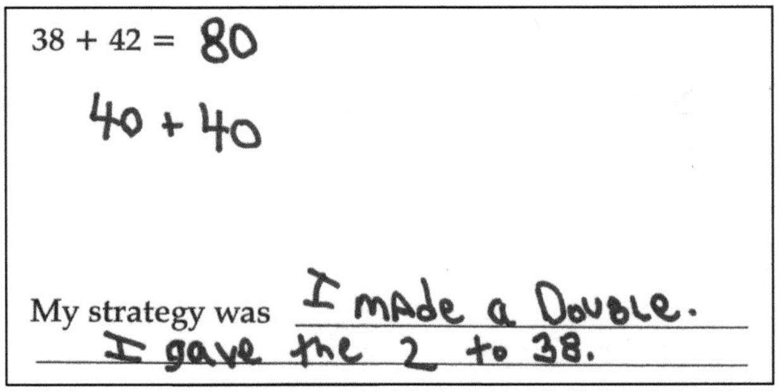

38 + 42 = 80
40 + 40
My strategy was I made a Double. I gave the 2 to 38.

Figure 2

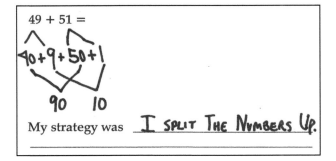

49 + 51 =
40 + 9 + 50 + 1
90 10
My strategy was I SPLIT THE NUMBERS UP.

Figure 3

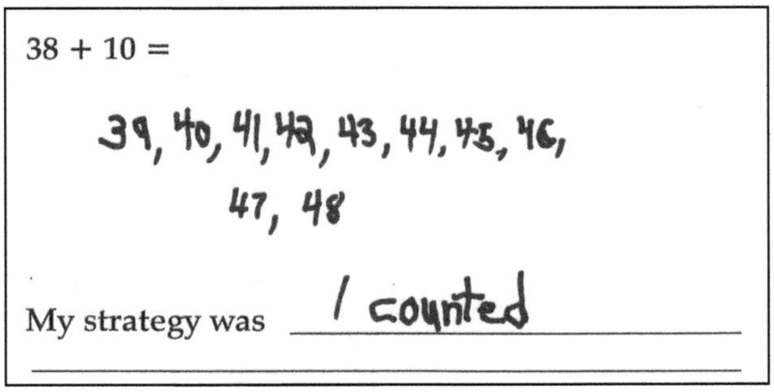

38 + 10 =
39, 40, 41, 42, 43, 44, 45, 46, 47, 48
My strategy was I counted

Figure 4

Reflections on the Day

As this unit nears completion, reflect on all the addition strategies you have witnessed the children discussing and using. Also reflect on how the open number line emerged as a class model as you worked through this unit. Now that it is a model children understand, you can use it throughout the year to continue to support addition and subtraction strategies. Over time you will begin to see children using it themselves as a tool to think with—to explore relations, such as the connection between addition and subtraction.

Celebrating the Art Show

Today is a day for celebration and a chance for your young mathematicians to share what they have been doing and learning. You will be having an art show for visitors and reading the class book you have put together.

It is helpful to document for the community the progression and completion of a unit with samples of children's ideas and samples of their work. The class book you made provides this documentation, including how children's ideas changed over time. Having a real art show also grounds the math investigations of the last two weeks in an authentic context.

The Celebration

Invite parents, the principal, and interested others to come to the art show. At the show, read the big book you have put together explaining the math you have done. The children can now serve as experts to help other children in the school do a similar project.

Materials Needed

Class book created on Day Nine

Children's art pieces, with signs, displayed in an area such as the art room, cafeteria, hallway, or library

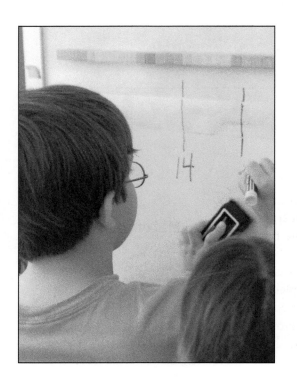

Reflections on the Unit

The mathematician Samuel Karlin (1983) once wrote, "The purpose of models is not to fit the data but to sharpen the questions." This unit supported the development of the number line as a powerful model for sharpening questions about number relations and operations. Starting with a measurement context, the model emerged from a blueprint with marks for cutting (a model of a situation) to a model used to represent computation strategies. As the unit progressed, the string of cubes was exchanged for a measurement tool composed of ten-strips, and double-digit addition strategies were represented on it. Eventually the measurement tool became an open number line. This model can now be used throughout the year as you continue to work on addition and subtraction. Another unit in this series, *Minilessons for Extending Addition and Subtraction*, can be a helpful resource as you continue to plan strings of related problems for minilessons and use the open number line to record children's strategies.

Tamika just loved school this year! She was in second grade and she loved it because she had the best teacher ever— Mrs. Washington!

Mrs. Washington loved math, just like Tamika, and she liked to organize fund-raisers for the school. "Community projects," she would call them.

"It takes a village," she would say. Tamika didn't really know what Mrs. Washington meant until last year when she organized a book fair. Lots of people came and bought books, and the school made lots of money. The principal used the money to buy new books for the school library.

"We came together like a village," Mrs. Washington had said with a satisfied smile, "and look what we accomplished."

This year Mrs. Washington was organizing an art fair. All the kids in the school had made lots of paintings, and Mrs. Washington had asked Tamika, Shaun, and Jaleelah to stay after school to help.

"We'll make a sign for each of the paintings," Jaleelah said.

"And very carefully," Tamika added as she went for the scissors. "We'll measure every painting and cut signs just the exact size of each painting."

Mrs. Washington opened up the closet door. Artwork was piled right up to the ceiling!

"Oh, no!" Tamika and Jaleelah groaned.

Mrs. Washington looked overwhelmed.

"We'll never finish!" Shaun said exactly what everyone was feeling.

That night when Tamika went home, she told her mom about the big pile of art, about all the work they had to do, and about what Shaun had said.

"I have an idea," her mom said. "Make it a class math project. Get the whole class to measure and then make a blueprint. If you do the measuring and the blueprint, I'll call some of the families and we'll cut out all the signs."

"What's a blueprint?" Tamika asked. She couldn't imagine what her mom was talking about.

"Like a plan with measurements on it. Something that shows us where to cut," her mom explained.

Tamika thought and thought. How could they make a blueprint? When she went to bed that night she was still thinking and then all of a sudden she had an idea.

In the morning she asked her mom, who was an accountant, for a roll of paper, the kind she used in her adding machine. Tamika put the roll of paper in her backpack and then she ran all the way to school. She couldn't wait to tell Mrs. Washington and Shaun and Jaleelah!

"My mom said the families would help if we measure and make a blueprint," Tamika said excitedly when she got to school.

She showed the roll of paper to Mrs. Washington, Shaun, and Jaleelah. "We can use this. We'll make a blueprint. The whole class can measure the artwork with cubes and we'll make marks on here. It'll be like a pattern that shows exactly how long to make the signs. My mom will call some of the families, and they will cut out the signs."

Mrs. Washington began to smile. Soon she was grinning. "A real community project," she said. "A village! We'll all do it together!" And so that day when it was time for math, Mrs. Washington pulled out all the artwork from the closet.

"Let's sort them all by size," Jaleelah said. They put the art into piles by sizes and then they measured each size with cubes to see how long they were.

Tamika rolled out the paper her mom had given her and taped it to the chalkboard. Above it she made a string of cubes so they would know where to make the marks once everything was measured.

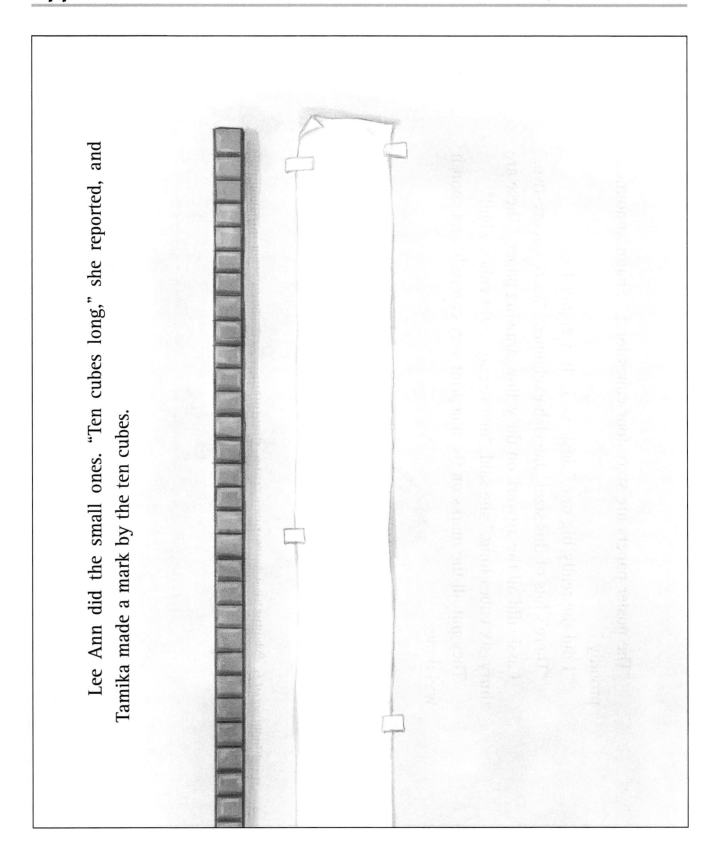

Lee Ann did the small ones. "Ten cubes long," she reported, and Tamika made a mark by the ten cubes.

"The poster papers are sixty-four cubes long," Shaun announced proudly.

"I did the really big one," Josie said. "It is eighty-four!"

"There's lots of this size!" Jaleelah exclaimed. "Mark twenty-two."

Cassie did all the artwork on the yellow drawing paper. "These are thirty-six cubes long," she said, "and twenty-eight cubes wide!"

They put all the marks on the blueprint very carefully and soon it was done.

That night, Tamika brought the blueprint home to her mom, and the next day the families used it to cut out all the signs.

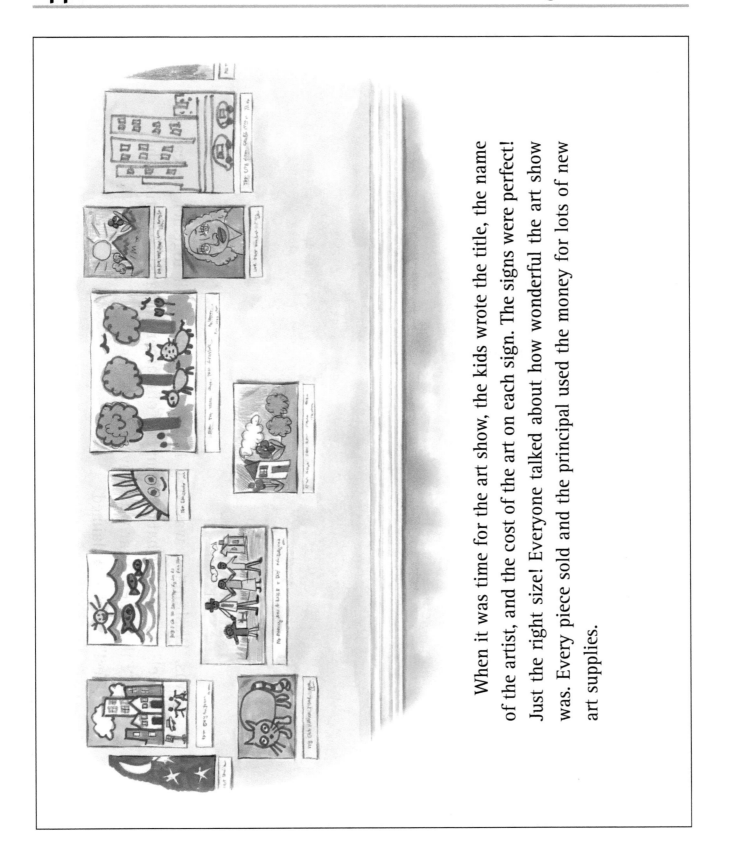

When it was time for the art show, the kids wrote the title, the name of the artist, and the cost of the art on each sign. The signs were perfect! Just the right size! Everyone talked about how wonderful the art show was. Every piece sold and the principal used the money for lots of new art supplies.

Mrs. Washington was very happy. "We did it all together, a real village!" she said. "What a community of mathematicians!" And then she said, "I think next year we'll have a math fair!"

"Yes!" Tamika exclaimed.

Names _____ Date _____

Blue paper:

Short side_____   Long side _____

Purple paper:

Short side_____   Long side _____

White paper:

Short side_____   Long side _____

Chart paper:

Short side_____   Long side _____

Yellow poster paper:

Short side_____   Long side _____

(for use with three-quarter-inch connecting cubes)

Tape	Tape	Tape	Tape	Tape

Appendix C

Strips of ten

(for use with two-centimeter connecting cubes)

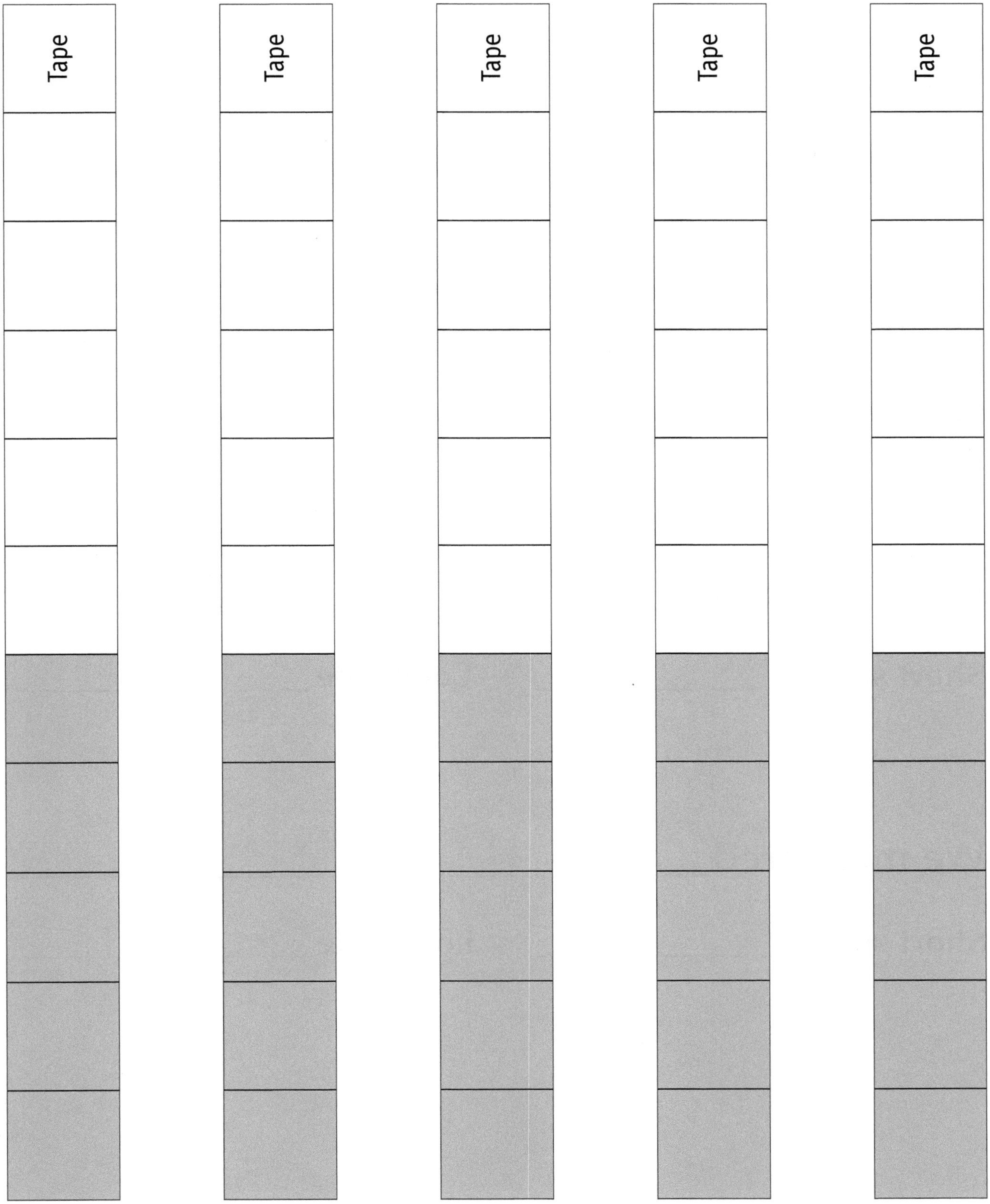

Tape
Tape
Tape
Tape
Tape

Names _____ Date _____

We measured_____

Short side _____   Long side_____

We measured_____

Short side _____   Long side_____

We measured_____

Short side _____   Long side_____

We measured_____

Short side _____   Long side_____

Names _____ Date _____

Paper	Measurement	Total
2 blue, short side	10 + 10	20
2 blue, long side	14 + 14	
2 purple, short side	20 + 20	
2 purple, long side	22 + 22	
2 white, short side	35 + 35	
2 white, long side	40 + 40	
2 chart paper, short side	46 + 46	
2 chart paper, long side	54 + 54	

■ These cards and the gameboard can be made more durable by pasting them on oaktag and laminating them.

Leap 1 ten	Leap 2 tens	Leap 3 tens
Leap 1 ten	Leap 1 ten	Leap 2 tens
Leap 1 ten	Leap 2 tens	Leap 2 tens

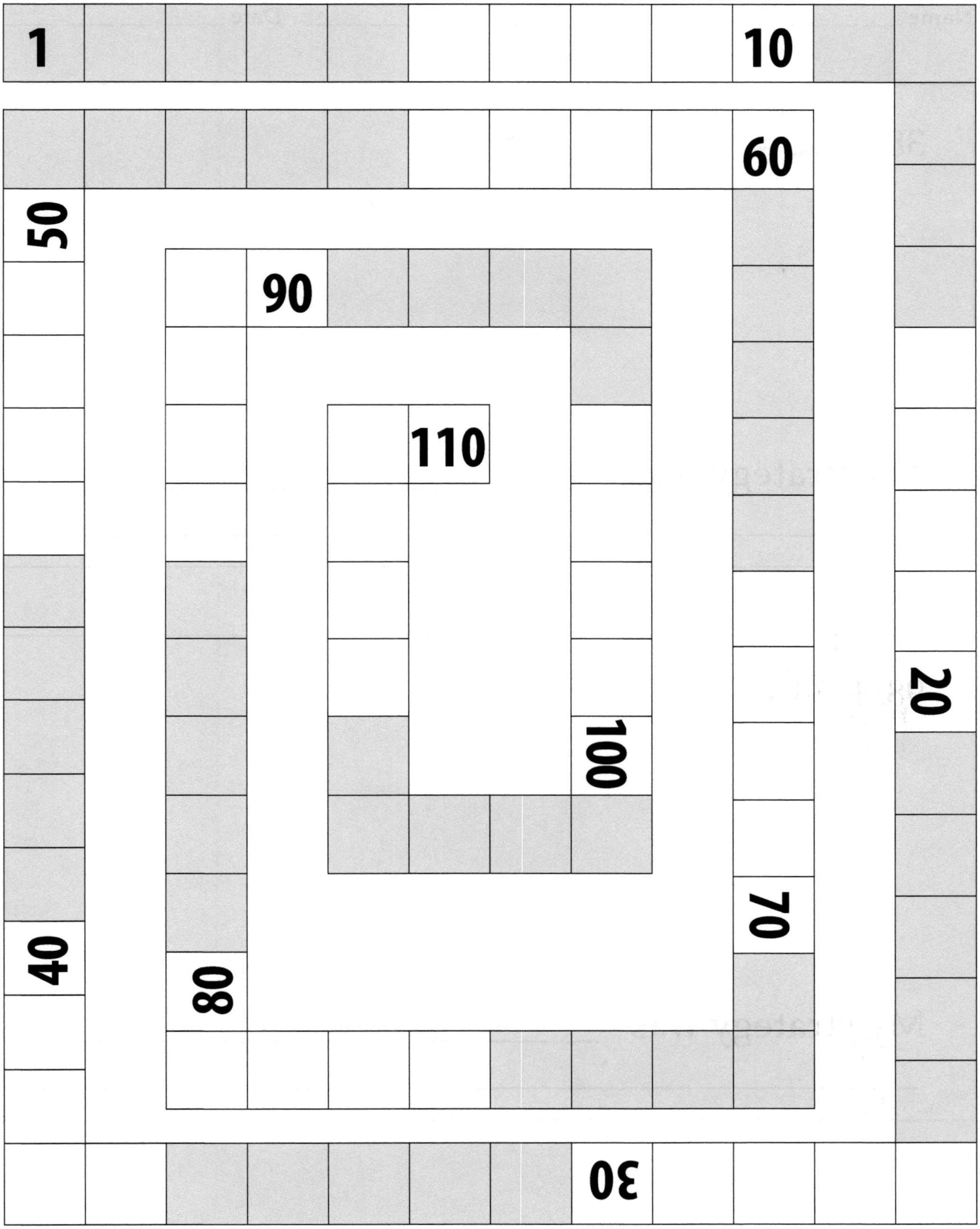
1
10
60
50
90
110
20
100
70
40
80
30

Student recording sheet for addition strategies

Name ______________________________ Date ______________

38 + 42 =

My strategy was ______________________________

____

98 + 34 =

My strategy was ______________________________

____

Student recording sheet for addition strategies

Name ______________________________ Date ______________

$38 + 10 =$

My strategy was ______________________________

____

$49 + 51 =$

My strategy was ______________________________

____